MACDOG'S DINNER

By Caroline and John Astrop

Firefly

Same old dog biscuits again.

I am going to find something new.

Cats love cream.

I don't.

Birds eat berries.

This is too tricky.

Sheep eat grass.

I don't like grass.

Ducks eat weed.

Horrible!

Rabbits eat carrots.

I'd rather dig up bones.

Cows love hay.

That looks more like a bed.

What do chickens eat?

I'm having a job pecking.

Hello mice, what's that stuff?

Cheese!!

I know what I like best.

Good old dog biscuits.

Let's talk about these pictures.

The mouse eats cheese. What do the others eat?

Hardback edition first published in the UK in 1989 by
Firefly Books Limited
61, Western Road, Hove
East Sussex BN3 1JD, England

British Library Cataloguing in Publication Data
Astrop, Caroline
Macdog's dinner.
I. Title II. Astrop, John III. Series
823'.914 (F)

ISBN 1 85485 030 X

Typeset by Type Practitioners, Sevenoaks, Kent
Printed in Italy

© Copyright Caroline and John Astrop 1989
Original paperback version published by Crocodile Books Ltd
1–6 Grand Parade, Brighton, East Sussex BN22 2QB